AI Is Taking Over The World

Jon Adams

Copyright © 2024 Jonathan Adams

All rights reserved.

ISBN: 9798877579415

CONTENTS

1 The Roots of Automation...Pg 7

2 AI The Brain Behind Automation................................Pg 17

3 Automation in the Workplace.......................................Pg 28

4 Everyday Life on Autopilot..Pg 35

5 Ethical and Social Considerations ....Pg 42

6 The Economic Implications of Automation ....Pg 58

7 The Future is Automated..Pg 73

INTRODUCTION

Welcome to 'AI Is Taking Over The World,' a prescient guide through the intricate landscape of modern automation and artificial intelligence. As you turn these pages, embark on an exploratory journey to understand the burgeoning force of technology that quietly orchestrates vast swaths of our daily existence. From the assembly lines that stitch together our clothes to the digital assistants that schedule our appointments, automation has permeated our lives in a profound and, until now, largely inconspicuous manner.

This book is a probing examination of why automation is not just a trend but a sweeping revolution poised to redefine human society. We'll delve into the gears of AI's coming dominance, offering clear perspectives flowing from the sophisticated algorithms that beat us at our own games to the self-driving cars that promise to make our roads safer. We peel back the curtain on the elemental forces driving automation's relentless advance: the pursuit of efficiency, the allure of cost reduction, and the human desire to push the boundaries of what's possible.

As we cast an eye toward the horizon, this book will furnish you with an array of examples highlighting automation's embeddedness in our everyday lives. From financial markets moved by intelligent software to smart homes that learn our preferences to make life more comfortable, these stories illustrate the depth of automation's reach.

Filled with insights from leading experts, gripping case studies, and a forward-looking analysis, 'AI Is Taking Over The World' synthesizes the complex web of technological advancements into a digest that will arm you with knowledge.

Whether you're intrigued, concerned, or simply curious, this book will engage your mind, prompt you to question the status quo, and offer a compass for navigating the future landscape, where AI's influence is as ordinary as the air we breathe. Prepare to be informed, engaged, and inspired as you step into a world where automation does not just assist but increasingly commands the sphere of human activity.

THE ROOTS OF AUTOMATION

As we stand on the brink of technological frontiers, it is essential to peer over our shoulders and trace the lineage of automation back to its rudimentary origins. Imagine the ancient world, where human hands first set tools into motion with an intent to function independently, embodying the seeds of automation. It commenced with simple yet ingenious apparatuses such as water clocks, which harnessed the laws of nature to keep time without cease. Over the centuries, these ripples of innovation coalesced into a surge of transformative potential, witnessed in the iconic automata of Heron of Alexandria, whose inventions seemed to breathe with a life of their own, and the pioneering programmable looms of Joseph Marie Jacquard that weaved intricate patterns at the bidding of perforated cards.

The mechanics of these early devices, while elementary by today's standards, laid bare the core principles of automation: the anticipation of a function, the delegation to a machine, and the repeatability of the task without falter in consistency. From steam engines that powered the industrial goliaths of the past to assembly lines that transformed the very fabric of manufacturing, these pillars have withstood the test of time. Each breakthrough served as a stepping stone that elevated the simplicity of mechanical automation to the sophistication of digital orchestration we see today.

As we unravel the intricacies of automation's past, we discover a narrative that is not just about gears, pulleys, and punch cards, but rather about humanity's enduring pursuit to harness time, increase efficiency, and expand our capabilities. The endeavor of early innovators echoes in modern corridors, where artificial intelligence and robotics continue to redefine possibility. With a discerning eye, we can foresee how the past informs our future, and in this knowledge, we find both a foundation and a launchpad for what is yet to come. Every chapter in the saga of automation aligns with the rhythm of human progress, a testament to our collective ingenuity and a beacon guiding us toward untrodden paths ripe for discovery.

In the pantheon of automation, few figures stand out more prominently than Heron of Alexandria, a true innovator whose work laid the groundwork for mechanized motion. Imagine, if you will, a device powered by steam, crafted in antiquity; this was the aeolipile, Heron's creation, which spun with vigorous energy harnessed from heated water. His automated temple doors, too, mystified onlookers by seemingly opening of their own accord, yet they were activated by a series of weights and counterbalances hidden from view, a clever manipulation of physics to achieve a desired effect without direct human intervention.

Fast forward through time to Al-Jazari, a polymath who took automatons to new heights with his intricate designs and ingenious contraptions. His Book of Knowledge of Ingenious Mechanical Devices speaks volumes of a man whose creativity knew no bounds, from musicians who played without a maestro to water clocks that operated with remarkable precision. Al-Jazari's work was more than just occupation of idle hands; it was a dialogue with the potential of the nonliving to mimic the living, a concept that inches closer to the paradigms of modern automation.

Then, in the shadows of the Industrial Revolution, emerged a figure whose contributions stitched together the realms of textile and technology: Joseph Marie Jacquard. His loom, a masterpiece of its time, utilized punch cards - a forerunner to modern binary code - to dictate patterns with such accuracy that it revolutionized fabric production. It wasn't merely a machine but a translator of human intent into tangible output through the elegant ballet of needles and threads.

These pioneers did not merely contribute gadgets to the annals of history; they each marked pivotal checkpoints in the long race of progress, challenging subsequent generations to reimagine the breadth of what could be automated. Their legacy is etched into the cavernous halls of innovation, setting a precedent for those who wish to push the boundaries of possibility, not with reckless abandon but with thoughtful precision and a gaze firmly fixed on the horizon of human potential. Their lives beckon us to consider the fusion of creativity and practicality, a synergy that propels technology forward and keeps the core of automation both robust and ever-evolving.

The water clock, or clepsydra, stands as one of the earliest triumphs in the story of automation. It operated on a principle of consistent water flow, either out of or into a vessel, with marked intervals to indicate the passage of time. An expertly calibrated trickle translated the invisible, relentless march of seconds and minutes into a visual and measurable display. Consider a transparent container, incrementally etched, with water levels descending or rising to mark the hours; this primeval clock emulates the very rhythm of nature, narrating time without a whisper or the need for human interference.

Turning the pages of history to the steam engine, we encounter a device that was once the heartbeat of the Industrial Revolution. At its core, the steam engine converts heat into mechanical work. Picture, if you will, the fervor of boiling water producing steam, this steam then expands, applying pressure. This force is harnessed and channeled, pushing pistons with mighty thrusts, turning wheels that set the world into motion. It showcased one of the earliest implementations of feedback control systems; governors were used to regulate speed, leading to consistent and safe operations.

The punch card system, introduced by Joseph Marie Jacquard, brought programmability into play, a concept inextricable from modern computing. These cards held patterns of holes, each corresponding to a particular design to be woven by the loom. As the cards passed through a reading mechanism, a binary choice was made: needles either passed through a hole, activating a hook to select a thread, or encountered solid card, leaving the hook at rest. This sequence of actions, determined by the patterned punch cards, dictated the intricate weavings without the manual adjustments traditionally made by the weaver. It laid the groundwork for the storied punch card computing that would come to be essential in the nascent days of computer science.

Finally, we arrive at the assembly line, a paradigm that fundamentally altered the ethos of manufacturing. On these lines, products move from station to station, with each worker or robot responsible for a specific, repetitive task. Within this orchestrated flow lies an early form of automation, the division and synchronization of labor to improve speed and efficiency while minimizing error. Visualize a conveyor belt in ceaseless motion, carrying pieces destined to become a whole under the careful hands or robotic arms that await at each chapter of the construction ballet.

Each of these historical devices and methodologies, from the water clock's passive reckoning of time to the steam engine's forceful conversion of heat to labor, and from the Jacquard loom's proto-programming to the relentless tempo of the assembly line, stands as proof of humanity's ceaseless quest to impose order on chaos, predictability on the erratic, and precision on the approximate. In their mechanics lie the echoes of modern automata, the grand tapestry of automation composed thread by thread, gear by gear, with the same principles guiding today's algorithms and robotics.

Examining the classic water clock, one must first comprehend the flow regulator's crucial role. The flow regulator, a variable orifice or gate, operates by limiting the volume of water either entering or exiting the clock's main chamber. Imagine the internal chamber as the timekeeper, where water enters or leaves at a pre-calibrated rate. The consistent drip or flow is paramount; it's the drumbeat of the clock's march through time. If one were to visualize, the flow regulator could take the form of an adjustable spigot that, when tightened, reduces the aperture through which the water flows, ensuring a steady, controlled release to mark time accurately.

Advance, then, to the governor of the steam engine, an elegant feedback system utilizing what is known as centrifugal force and the outward force experienced by an object moving in a circular path. Picture two arms with weighted balls at each end, connected to a central spindle driven by the engine's output. As engine speed increases, so does the spinning of these balls, and they move outward, triggering a linkage to reduce the steam valve's opening. This action limits the steam inflow, thus decreasing engine speed, a self-regulating mechanism ensuring stability and safety.

Shift focus now to the punch card system, an early incarnation of programmed instruction. The Jacquard loom, for instance, utilized punch cards with rows of strategically placed holes that corresponded to a textile pattern. As each card passed over a series of needles, those aligned with holes would drop through, engaging a hook mechanism. This hook then raised the correct thread for the weft. In the absence of a hole, the needle remained stationary, and the thread stayed lowered. This binary choice - hole or no hole, hook or rest - allowed for complex patterns to be reproduced with precision and efficiency, an embryonic glimpse at what would evolve into computer programming.

Lastly, consider the choreography of an assembly line, where timing and sequence are imperative. Each workstation has a distinct start and end point for its task, synchronized to the movement of the production line. Think of a grand clock, where the second hand's every tick signals the change from one step to the next, all components coming together in a fluid and methodical cadence. The timing belts and rotary tables revolve in concert, each segment of the process carefully metered to coincide with the next. It's a ballet of mechanical precision, where human and robotic participants are integrated into an intricate dance of progress, ensuring the harmonious creation of a final product.

In each system, from the regulating flow of the water clock to the spinning governors of steam engines, from the binary selection of punch cards to the tempo of assembly lines, one finds a rhythmic pattern of meticulous design and control. These devices, grounded in physics and buoyed by human ingenuity, form the historical tapestry of automation, each thread a narrative of progress leading to the machines that shape our modern world.

Travel through history and you'll find marvels of innovation, marking the path to our present landscape of technology. Ancient automata, mechanical figures expertly crafted by the likes of Heron of Alexandria, performed actions that mimicked the living. One might envision these early robots as performers on a stage, following a script laid down by gears and levers, executing tasks with a precision that seemed almost magical to onlookers. They were the nascent inklings of AI's pedigree, exemplars of physical tasks programmed by human foresight and mechanical arrangement.

In the same breath, speak of the programmable loom, a historical linchpin marrying the textile craft with coded instructions long before the digital age took hold. The Jacquard loom, with its intricate dance of needles responding to punch cards, transformed patterns into woven fabric. Its process intensifies under scrutiny, revealing an echo of the very logic that underpins modern programming languages and a series of binary decisions creating complex outcomes.

Then observe the assembly line, perhaps the most telling forebear of modern production. The concept of standardization introduced by Henry Ford enacted a symphony of efficiency, each worker a musician, each role precisely timed. This choreography of tasks imparts a legacy of optimization and consistency that is now orchestrated by the deft "hands" of robotic counterparts in factories worldwide.

Thus, from the sophistication of ancient mechanics to the foresight of early programming and the systematization of the production line, the lineage is clear. These endeavors sculpted a framework for today's artificial intelligence and robotics, a testament to human ingenuity's relentless momentum. While the technologies of yesteryear had their limitations, bound by the materials and knowledge of their time, they laid down the axioms that inform, even today, the continually advancing field of automation. Such a contemplation lends the modern observer not only an understanding of the technical underpinnings but also an appreciation for the persistence of innovation's intricate dance across the ages.

Gaze upon today's technological marvels - intricate networks that span the globe, machines that ponder vast data sets and posit solutions, robotic limbs that perform with a surgeon's precision. To understand these feats, one must journey to the foundries of the past, where early automation practices were the forge and anvil upon which the future was hammered out. It began with rudimentary tools, elemental in design, that functioned autonomously - a promise of what might be if human intellect and mechanical potential converged.

These historical innovations, while elemental, encapsulated profound principles: the consistency of water clocks that instilled a sense of time's passage without human upkeep, the programmable loom's punch cards that prefigured digital code, or the assembly line's testament to process and efficiency. They served not as endpoints but as portals to uncharted realms of possibility, limitations of their age notwithstanding.

The legacy these practices bestow runs deep through contemporary technology, instilling an architectural lineage - a common DNA in the shape of algorithmic thought, structural integrity, feedback loops, and operational efficiencies. Even as materials and methods advanced, the lineage of ideas remained robust, compelling the latest advancements to follow the contours laid by ancestral hands.

As one contemplates this heritage, there is an awakening to the realization that today's silicon and software are born from yesteryear's gears and cogs. A reader today, equipped with an understanding of this progression, can appreciate not only the sophistication of current systems but also the resolute creativity that bridged eras. The same drive to expand human capacity, which once carved channels for water to measure the hours, now architects neural networks that learn and evolve. The discourse on these matters, stripped of jargon and inflated rhetoric, is a vivid reminder: progress is the child of necessity and ingenuity, cradled in the hands of those who dare to dream and toil, echoing from the workshops of ancient tinkerers to the laboratories of modern innovators.

Within this chapter's pages, we have traced the arc of automation's ascent from the earliest water clocks to the sophisticated systems defining our era. Each story, from Heron's automata to Jacquard's loom, from Ford's assembly line to contemporary robotics, forms a tessellation of incremental progress. Through this journey, one is invited to appreciate the immutable constants at play: the persistence of human ingenuity, the inevitability of innovation born from necessity, and the transformative power of technology leveraged for efficiency and precision.

Understanding these cornerstones is not merely academic; it is a compass for navigating the potential and pitfalls of the future's automated landscape. Just as the first water clocks evolved into timepieces of stunning accuracy, so too will today's machines evolve, guided by the principles unearthed by their predecessors. In the finer mechanics of these early inventions lie the seeds of tomorrow's advancements and reminders that even the most extraordinary leaps in capability are rooted in a lineage of progress, each step resting upon the last.

One closes this chapter with an empowered grasp of automation's genesis, ready to explore the burgeoning frontiers ahead with a sensibility shaped by history. It is an understanding that will serve to demystify modern complexity, reducing seemingly intricate innovations into discernible, logical evolutions of what came before. There is a compelling continuity here: just as past innovators triumphed over the limitations of their tools, so will the visionaries of the present rise to meet the challenges of their time. In this spirit, one moves forward, not as a passive observer to the onrush of progress but as an informed participant, eager to contribute to the ongoing narrative of human endeavor.

AI THE BRAIN BEHIND AUTOMATION

In the sweep of technological evolution, artificial intelligence stands as a remarkable testament to human creativity and the pursuit of heightened capability. Born from the crucible of theoretical musings and mathematical models, AI has ascended from the abstract realm of possibility into the concrete world where it now orchestrates complex systems and processes with remarkable autonomy. The journey began with the conception of devices that could not only calculate but 'think' -- machines fashioned from the blueprint of human cognition yet unbound by the constraints of organic intellect.

At the heart of this evolution is the algorithm, a term that belies the intricate logic woven into its digital fabric. Algorithms serve as the building blocks for AI, designed to parse data, learn patterns, and make decisions that mimic the cognitive function -- a symphony of zeros and ones that riff on the notes of human reasoning. These lines of code graduate from mere instructions to become the pulse of a learning entity, capable of adapting and evolving through methods like machine learning and neural networks.

AI's seamless integration into the nervous system of industry -- from transport logistics that predict the ebb and flow of traffic, to healthcare algorithms diagnosing patients with a precision rivaling practitioners -- speaks to its transformative impact. Yet, with all its prowess, AI is not infallible. Bias in data, the opacity of decision-making processes, and a burgeoning menu of ethical quandaries remind us that this technology, though potent, is still an instrument fashioned by fallible hands.

As one contemplates the vast expanse of AI's influence, it is essential to recognize both the elegance of its design and the implications of its deployment. To understand AI is to hold a lens to the future, envisioning a horizon replete with opportunity yet requiring careful navigation. With each step along AI's developmental path, an invitation is extended to engage, not just as passive recipients but as shapers of an automated landscape where human and artificial intelligence converge. In this initiation, one finds not just the mechanics of a tool but the dynamism of a partner in the ceaseless endeavor to extend the reach of what is humanly possible.

In the nascent stages of computational logic, artificial intelligence operated within the confines of rule-based systems, where the scope of decision-making was tethered to a predetermined set of rules. These systems, although trailblazing for their time, lacked the ability to learn from data and adjust their operations dynamically. Enter the perceptron, a prototypical form of a neural network, conceived by Frank Rosenblatt as an analog to human cognition. Envision the perceptron as an elementary processor that, when presented with input data, weighs it, sums it, and then makes a binary decision: whether to activate an output signal, akin to the neurons firing in the human brain.

This binary output constitutes the perceptron's prediction, based simply on its current set of weights, which initially are random assignments. Learning occurs by adjusting these weights incrementally through repeated training cycles, a process starkly different from the static mappings within rule-based systems.

However, the perceptron's scope is limited and it cannot solve problems that aren't linearly separable, meaning it struggles with more complex patterns where a simple line can't separate different classes of inputs.

The true revolution came with the concept of backpropagation, an ingenious method employed in training deep learning models. Imagine a multilayered network of perceptrons, commonly known as a neural network, where after an incorrect output, the error is carried back through the layers. Through a mathematically rigorous process, each neuron in the network receives feedback on its contribution to the error, enabling it to adjust its weights in a way that minimizes the mistake for future predictions. It is akin to a highly coordinated team debrief after a failed project, where every member analyzes and amends their actions to ensure better outcomes in future endeavors.

This backpropagation protocol is a cornerstone of deep learning, a subset of AI that employs complex neural networks capable of identifying intricate and abstract patterns within vast data sets. It allows machines to learn and adapt with human-like flexibility, surpassing the capacity of traditional rule-based systems. By forging connections and identifying patterns within massive volumes of data, backpropagation imbues AI systems with a semblance of intuition, constructing a robust, adaptable framework that can revolutionize fields from vision recognition systems to natural language processing. Through this intricate dance of predictive correction, artificial intelligence has made a seismic shift from rigid, rule-bound operators to fluid, learning entities with an ever-expanding potential for complexity.

A neural network is a construct inspired by the human brain, consisting of layers of interconnected nodes or 'neurons' that work in unison to process information. This architecture typically includes an input layer, one or more hidden layers, and an output layer. Each neuron in these layers is connected to neurons in the subsequent layer through 'weights,' which are numerical values that influence the strength and direction of the signal between neurons. Additionally, each neuron has a 'bias,' a standalone parameter that allows the neuron to adjust its output independently.

Upon receiving an input, the network performs a 'forward pass.' During this phase, the input data is fed into the input layer, which then communicates to the hidden layers. As data moves from one layer to the next, the input to each neuron is calculated as a weighted sum of the outputs of the neurons from the previous layer, adjusted by the neuron's bias. The resulting value then undergoes a transformation via an 'activation function,' which determines the neuron's output signal to the next layer. This process repeats until the final output layer is reached, culminating in a prediction or classification made by the network.

Error evaluation follows the forward pass, where the network's output is compared to the desired target or actual value, quantifying the network's accuracy using a 'loss function.' This function assigns a numerical value to the error, with lower numbers representing better performance and higher numbers indicating greater error.

Backpropagation begins once the loss is computed. The core idea is to minimize the loss by adjusting the weights and biases, starting from the output and moving backward through the network and a propagation of error in reverse. To do this, the partial derivative of the loss function concerning each weight and bias is calculated, a discipline known as 'gradient descent.'

These derivatives provide the direction in which the weights and biases need to be adjusted to reduce the error.

The 'learning rate' is a hyperparameter that determines the step size during each iteration of weight updating. Think of it as the pace at which the network learns; too swift, and it may overshoot the optimal solution; too slow, and the training becomes inefficient.

The pseudo code for a simple backpropagation algorithm might look something like this:

```
initialize network weights and biases randomly
for each training example in data:
    perform forward pass to compute output
    calculate the loss comparing output to the target value
    perform backward pass to compute gradients using loss
    for each weight and bias in network:
        adjust weights and biases in the negative gradient direction, scaled by the learning rate
```

Backpropagation is iterative. With each pass through the training data, the neural network fine-tunes its weights and biases to reduce the loss, incrementally improving its predictions. The remarkable aspect of backpropagation lies in its ability to learn from errors, constantly refining the network's parameters until it can delineate patterns and insights from the data with high precision, emulating a form of learning that's both dynamic and nuanced.

Alan Turing, often hailed as the progenitor of artificial intelligence, laid the philosophical groundwork with a question that probes the heart of the discipline: Can machines think? His formulation of the Turing Test was instrumental in setting a benchmark for machine intelligence, challenging one to discern if a machine's responses are indistinguishable from that of a human's. Turing did not simply present a conundrum; he provided a framework for thinking about artificial cognizance, triggering a paradigm shift that would lead to computational models capable of simulating aspects of human thought.

Building on this transformative groundwork, Frank Rosenblatt introduced the perceptron, an attempt to mechanize the processes of the human brain within a computational model. The perceptron, as an initial representation of a neural network, offered a method for computers to process information and 'learn' by adjusting to patterns through its own exposure to data and essentially allowing a program to modify its behavior based on experience, akin to a rudimentary form of adaptation.

Enter Geoffrey Hinton, decades later, whose pivotal contributions to the field of neural network research catalyzed the deep learning renaissance. Hinton's exploration of backpropagation and relentless belief in the power of neural networks unearthed the potential for machines to decipher complex, hierarchical patterns through layers of processing, a stark departure from the linear computations of early models. This shift paved the way for contemporary AI's ability to tackle intricate tasks from recognizing speech to interpreting medical images and with a proficiency that sometimes mirrors and even surpasses human capability.

Each of these luminaries contributed layers to the intricate mosaic of AI, from Turing's philosophical and computational foundations to Rosenblatt's nascent models of neuronal activity, culminating in Hinton's tenacious pursuit of advanced neural network architectures and a lineage of innovation that has progressively dismantled the barriers between the methodical realm of the machine and the fluid world of human intellect.

In the realm of manufacturing, the advent of AI has signaled a profound shift from the traditional reactive approach to a proactive methodology known as predictive maintenance. This concept, although seemingly straightforward, revolutionizes the maintenance protocol by forecasting equipment failure before it occurs. It is enabled through the continuous monitoring of machine conditions, wherein AI algorithms analyze data trends to detect subtle anomalies, patterns, and correlations that may elude human scrutiny.

Consider an AI system that tracks the vibration patterns of an industrial pump; by learning what constitutes the baseline operational 'hum,' the AI can discern the slightest deviation predictive of a future malfunction. This application of AI not only constitutes a leap in ensuring operational integrity but also stands as a bulwark against unplanned outages and the associated downtime costs.

It represents a strategic pivot to a maintenance schedule that is dictated not by arbitrary timelines or haphazard failures but informed by the precise intelligence gleaned from actual equipment status. This migration from a stance of repair after failure to one of informed anticipation brings with it enhanced efficiency, as resources are allocated with discernment, and productivity, as machines sustain optimal uptime with minimized interruption.

Though the sophistication of this technology promises extensive benefits, one must also acknowledge potential limitations, such as the necessity for substantial data for accurate forecasting and the complexity of integrating AI systems into existing infrastructures. Nevertheless, the promise of AI in transforming maintenance from a guessing game into a science of certainty offers a compelling narrative of progress for industries where peak performance is paramount.

In the vanguard of artificial intelligence, thought leaders like Stuart Russell cast a spotlight on the ethical dimensions of this powerful technology, asserting the crucial need for AI to be developed with human values and societal well-being at its core. The foundational idea is that AI, a tool with profound potential, must be aligned with the very moral and ethical principles that underpin human civilization. Russell advocates for a framework wherein AI systems are not only robust in their capabilities but also, and more importantly, beneficial in their impact.

To operationalize such an ethic-centric approach, one must first define the values that the AI is to uphold a task as critical as it is complex, given the rich tapestry of cultural and individual diversity. The framework pursued by Russell and like-minded advocates demands meticulous design, where algorithms must be programmed to consider the plethora of consequences their actions may have, extending far beyond the immediate task at hand. These AI systems must be developed under the guiding star of beneficence, preventing harm and amplifying human welfare, while ensuring their autonomous decision-making processes do not inadvertently contravene ethical standards.

This investigation into ethical AI is not just philosophical rumination; it bears tangible implications for everything from autonomous vehicles to financial algorithms, where the decisions of AI can have material effects on human lives. The sophistication of such systems demands an equally sophisticated understanding of ethics, a balanced approach that recognizes the responsibility borne by creators and operators to instill AI with a compass that reliably points toward humanity's collective moral north. After all, the integration of AI into the societal fabric is not simply a matter of technological achievement but an exercise in conscientious craftsmanship, ensuring its threads strengthen rather than unravel the societal tapestry.

Visionaries like Demis Hassabis peer into the future of artificial intelligence with a lens calibrated to the possibilities of general-purpose AI and a concept reaching beyond the specialized functions of today's AI applications. Picture a tool not just sharpened for a single task, but a versatile instrument capable of adapting to a multitude of roles. The crux of this innovation rests in designing AI systems that do not simply excel in a siloed discipline, but possess the intellectual dexterity to apply their learning across a broad spectrum of domains.

Hassabis, co-founder of DeepMind, maps the trajectory of AI as moving toward an epoch where machines can learn and reason with a generality that echoes human cognition. Such a leap from the present landscape, where AI systems are highly skilled yet narrowly focused, to one of general-purpose AI entails the formidable challenge of cultivating algorithms with the ability to transfer knowledge from one context to another is akin to a master key unlocking diverse doors of understanding.

The implications are profound, suggesting automated systems could dynamically adjust to new tasks with minimal human intervention. Imagine a future where AI could navigate the nuances of healthcare diagnostics just as adeptly as it manages financial markets, or maneuvers autonomous vehicles.

Yet, with this breadth comes the need for caution in development, ensuring such systems can discern ethical boundaries and operate within the parameters of societal norms.

Understanding general-purpose AI demands a recognition of the balance between its transformative potential and the meticulous groundwork required to actualize it. This new horizon, painted by Hassabis and thinkers alike, postulates not only a revolution in the capability of automated systems but also an evolution in the symbiotic relationship between AI and human endeavor, one that could redefine the landscape of human achievement.

As this discourse on the essence and trajectory of artificial intelligence concludes, one is compelled to acknowledge AI's indelible role as the linchpin of modern automation. The technology that simulates human thought processes, learns from vast troves of data, and makes decisions with increasing autonomy has firmly entrenched itself within the bedrock of contemporary systems. To understand the implications of AI is to wield a compass that points toward the intricacies of progress; it allows one to navigate a rapidly shifting landscape where advancements in this field become the beacons that redefine our interaction with machines.

A meticulous examination of AI's progression from its embryonic state to today's sophisticated algorithms reveals a consistent trend of expansion in capability and reach. With each leap forward, it's as though a new language of possibility is penned, granting machines a fluency in tasks once thought the sole province of human expertise. Yet, for all its promise, a keen awareness of AI's limitations serves as a sobering counterbalance, reminding us that this technology, potent as it may be, is a creation of fallible humanity and thus subject to oversight and guidance.

The future vistas of AI's influence are replete with as yet unconquered peaks and horizons waiting to be explored. As one contemplates the transitions ahead, it becomes clear that a profound comprehension of AI not only enhances one's readiness for what is to come but also engenders a sense of empowerment to shape the future trajectory of this extraordinary technological symphony. The shared journey with AI is one not merely of adaptation but of co-evolution but an engagement with our own creations that will persistently sculpt the narrative of human ingenuity.

AUTOMATION IN THE WORKPLACE

At the heart of the modern work environment thrives a phenomenon known as automation, a term that encapsulates an array of technologies bound by the common thread of minimizing human intervention in tasks. This trend is by no means homogeneous; it comprises robotic process automation (RPA), which automates routine digital tasks, artificial intelligence (AI) that simulates cognitive functions such as problem-solving, and physical robotics that replace or augment human efforts in the material world.

As this chapter unfolds, one will discover the tapestry of automation's influence on the workplace, woven from threads as varied as the technologies themselves. RPA, for instance, streamlines workflows, whereas AI extends into the realms of decision-making and data analysis. Physical robotics transforms manufacturing floors and logistics, enhancing precision and efficiency. These components of automation converge in the modern workplace, blending the mechanical precision of robots with the subtlety of AI algorithms to reforge the nature of labor and industry.

However, the landscape sculpted by automation is not without its crevasses and peaks. While unlocking new horizons of productivity, these technologies prompt reevaluation of the skills valuable in the workforce and echo questions about the future of human labor. It is here, at this intersection of potential and precaution, that this discourse aims to guide the reader, offering not just a map of where automation has led the workforce thus far, but also a compass to navigate the shifting terrain it has yet to shape. In examining the sinews of automation's impact on work, one gains not just awareness but an empowerment to adapt and thrive in the rhythm of progress that automation invariably conducts.

Robotic Process Automation, or RPA, is akin to an indefatigable office clerk, replicating keystrokes and mouse clicks to perform repetitive tasks, such as data entry or invoice processing. By interacting with user interfaces in the same manner a person would, RPA tools carry out assigned procedures, compiling reports or managing records with unerring accuracy and speed. One finds that in the financial sector, for instance, RPA swiftly reconciles transactions, liberating human workers from the tedium of balancing ledgers.

Artificial Intelligence, the broader and more intricate cousin of RPA, does not simply replicate tasks but learns to optimise them. Through AI, machines are employing complex algorithms to parse through volumes of data, offering insights and decisions at a velocity and depth unmatchable by human capability. It is in customer service operations that AI's might shines brightly; chatbots, powered by natural language processing, engage with clients, addressing inquiries with an efficiency that transforms customer experience.

Physical robotics, on the manufacturing floor, articulates a symphony of automated tasks, from welding metal frames to assembling electronic components. These robotics systems blend precision sensors, actuators, and advanced control systems to perform physical activities that exceed human dexterity or stamina. In healthcare, robotic systems assist in surgeries, their metallic arms executing incisions and sutures with microscopic precision that enhances patient outcomes.

Each of these technologies like RPA, AI, and physical robotics contributes uniquely to the workplace, offering not just labor substitution, but augmentation. They automate tasks, present data-driven insights, and perform complex physical operations with consistent excellence. Yet as one marvels at their prowess, it is prudent to remember the vast resources and ingenuity required to train, maintain and integrate these systems into the flow of work. The result is a relentless advance toward a workplace that marries the strengths of machine with the irreplaceable creative and emotional intelligence of humans.

The historical tapestry of workplace automation is woven from a myriad of threads, each representing a leap forward in the effort to enhance productivity and precision. The narrative begins with early mechanical aids, such as the Jacquard loom, which transformed textile manufacturing by automating the pattern process via punch cards. This innovation laid a rudimentary groundwork for computational thinking, prefiguring the mechanization that would later permeate the industrial sphere.

As time progressed, researchers and innovators like Henry Ford conceived assembly lines that redefined manufacturing efficiency, instigating a new era where human labor was synchronized with mechanical rhythm. The trajectory of innovation soared with the advent of electronic machines, as seen in the work of Norbert Wiener, whose studies on cybernetics underpinned the principles of automated control systems.

The digital age ushered in groundbreaking computational models, with pioneers like Alan Turing, who advanced the concept of machines that could simulate analytical processes akin to the human mind. It was from Turing's prescient foundations that the field of artificial intelligence burgeoned, growing into the sophisticated AI systems in today's workplaces. The work of contemporary thought leaders, such as Andrew McAfee and Erik Brynjolfsson, explores this symbiosis of machine learning and human labor, offering critical insights into the economic and social dynamics shaped by such integration.

In examining the lineage from mechanical looms to learning algorithms, the evolution of workplace automation emerges as a reflection of human inventiveness, marked by a continual striving for systems that complement and amplify the capacities of workers. While each advance promises increased efficiency, it also necessitates an understanding of the implications that such shifts entail for the nature of work itself. Thus, one comes to perceive automation not as a static endpoint, but as a continuum of invention, where each development, while animated by the pursuit of productivity, is equally shaped by the human context in which it resides.

In the examination of automation's impact on employment, one can look to the automotive industry, where robotic arms that weld and assemble are now fixtures on the factory floor. Such advancements have led to the displacement of certain manual jobs, renowned for their repetitious and physically demanding nature. Conversely, this same shift has precipitated the need for robot technicians, programmers, and engineers, roles that necessitate a higher level of education and technical acumen. Another illustrative case is the financial sector's adoption of machine learning algorithms for data analysis and fraud detection. Here, the displacement narrative is accompanied by the emergence of data scientists and analysts who are skilled in guiding these intelligent systems to discern patterns and hazards previously imperceptible to the human eye.

The health care industry provides yet another perspective, where the deployment of AI for diagnostic purposes complements medical professionals. While AI does not replace doctors, it augments their capabilities, which, in turn, propels an increasing demand for AI specialists capable of bridging the chasm between machine intelligence and medical expertise.

Each case underscores a common theme: the twin narrative of job displacement coupled with the advent of new, often more sophisticated, forms of employment. While the initial focus revolves around jobs lost to automation, it is equally important to recognize the landscape of opportunities spawned by such technological disruption and a landscape that requires adaptation, reskilling, and a vision that sees beyond the horizon of the present into the emergent future of work.

The interplay between automation and the economy unfolds on a grand scale, with workforce dynamics at the vortex of this transformative storm. An array of studies, including those by the World Economic Forum, present a narrative where automation not only redistributes labor across sectors but also reshapes the very essence of work. The proliferation of automation ushers in heightened productivity and economic growth, yet it also stirs the waters of employment with the undercurrent of job displacement, particularly for roles that entail routine and manual tasks.

As machines and algorithms take on these roles with increasing prowess, the labor market sees a concurrent swell in demand for technical, managerial, and creative jobs and a reflection of tasks that require a distinctly human touch. This shift predicates a dual narrative: on one hand, a reduction in some forms of employment; on the other, an emergence of opportunities calling for new skill sets and competencies.

However, this transition is not without friction. The necessity for policy responses becomes clear as the gaps widen between the evolving demands of the workforce and the readiness of workers to meet them. Interventions such as reskilling programs, educational reforms, and support for displaced workers are paramount in aligning the gears of automation with the aspirations and welfare of the workforce. Policy responses entrenched in foresight can facilitate a harmonious evolution, where automation serves as a catalyst for empowerment and innovation rather than a source of socioeconomic rift. In navigating these unfolding dynamics, a well-charted course that considers the holistic implications of automation on society will not only inform but also equip those steering the economy for the undulating journey ahead.

The narrative of automation within the workplace is both a story of transformation and a blueprint for adaptation. At its inception, automation emerged as a mechanical support for human tasks, yet its trajectory veered sharply with the digital revolution, leading to complex systems capable of decisions and operations that once lay firmly in the realm of human intellect. As this trend marches forward, the augmentation of work with automated systems continues to blur the lines between tool and teammate.

A synthesis of insights from myriad fields presents a vision of automation as both disruptor and catalyst. For some, it represents a harbinger of obsolescence; for others, a beacon for new frontiers in professional development and employment.

The evolving nature of work creates a dynamic chessboard, where each move is predicated on anticipating the adaptability of both technology and human skill.

Understanding these shifts is not merely academic it is a vital compass that empowers all stakeholders, from policymakers to educators, from business leaders to workers themselves, to chart their course in this new landscape. With a discerning grasp of automation's capabilities and limitations, there emerges a framework to not just respond to change but to anticipate and shape it. For in the heart of these changes lies an opportunity: to forge a workforce that is resilient, diversified, and equipped with tools that are as intellectually robust as they are mechanically efficient. This clarity does not come from looking at automation as a challenge to employment but rather as an evolutionary step in the saga of work and one that handsomely rewards those who navigate its currents with foresight and agility.

EVERYDAY LIFE ON AUTOPILOT

The dawn of each day unfolds to the orchestration of automation, a term once confined to the lexicon of industry, now an intimate fixture in daily life. Consider the ubiquitous AI-powered alarm clock, which nudges one from slumber not with a mere ring, but with a dynamic understanding of sleep patterns and optimal waking times. Its operation, though silent and unseen, is the product of complex algorithms that analyze data to personalize the start of a day.

From this first interaction, the thread of automation weaves through the fabric of the day's routine. In the kitchen, coffee brews at the command of a smartphone, and in the living room, the news plays on a smart TV cued to personal preferences, all while the household's temperature adjusts itself in a quiet ballet of sensors and machine learning and learning thermostats gauging occupancy and ambient conditions to create comfort efficiently.

Stepping out the door, one may enter the domain of the self-driving car, an epitome of automation's advance. Here, radar, cameras, and AI converge to navigate the pulsing arteries of city traffic with a precision born from sophisticated programming and exhaustive data collection. This seamless blend of technology not only revolutionizes the commute but also extends the boundaries of personal freedom and safety.

Yet, as one marvels at the convenience and efficiency, it

becomes apparent that such systems are bound by the parameters of their programming, their functionality fenced by the current state of innovation and integration in society. The sophistication of these automated tools reflects a dual narrative of empowerment and ongoing ingenuity and a dance between technology's current prowess and the envisioned horizons it has yet to claim. It is this delicate balance that underscores the role of automation in daily life, casting new light on the ordinary, driving a renaissance of routine where the everyday is anything but.

Learning thermostats, a flagship innovation in the realm of smart home devices, harness a blend of sensors, algorithms, and user interface design to create an in-home climate that dynamically responds to its inhabitants. These thermostats observe user habits like preferred temperatures at various times of the day, or even times when the house is typically unoccupied and adjust heating and cooling systems accordingly. The environmental factors come into play through external data feeds that inform the device of local weather conditions, enhancing its ability to maintain comfort while optimizing energy use.

The mechanics of this process rest on the thermostat's ability to collect and analyze data, create a pattern-based profile, and make proactive adjustments. Data from motion sensors indicate presence or absence, while temperature sensors provide real-time feedback on the environment's state, feeding into a microprocessor that, through the use of machine learning, calibrates the system to operate with both efficiency and intuitiveness.

Despite the sophistication of these devices, limitations exist. The accuracy of learning thermostats can be constrained by the complexity of individual behaviors and variability in household dynamics. While the systems are designed to learn and adapt, there is an inherent delay in capturing new patterns, and external factors such as sudden weather shifts or unique user preferences can challenge their predictive capabilities.

Overall, the evolution of learning thermostats from rigid, schedule-based operations to adaptive, responsive systems epitomizes the potential of smart home technology. These devices not only represent a shift toward convenience and energy efficiency but also exemplify the iterative nature of innovation, where each advancement carves a path for further refinement and sophistication. It is within this continuum of development that such technology finds its stride, offering users a harmonious blend of comfort, control, and conservation.

In the vast expanse of Amazon's automated warehouses, a ballet of machinery and precision unfolds, underscoring the power of automation in logistics. Here, a fleet of robots glides across the floor, retrieving items and transporting them with efficiency that dwarfs human capability. Each robot is a cog in a grand machine, driven by algorithms that dictate its path and ensure seamless inventory management, all while minimizing the possibility of human error and fatigue.

Then there's Tesla's Autopilot, a feature that propels the discourse on personal transportation into the future. With an array of sensors and cameras in concert with sophisticated software, Tesla vehicles can navigate roads, interpret traffic signals, and react to dynamic driving scenarios. This symphony of hardware and software offers a glimpse into a potential future where the demands of focus and reaction time are alleviated from the driver. Although not fully autonomous, the Autopilot feature represents a significant stride toward the concept of self-driving vehicles, accentuating both the technological ingenuity and the stages of evolution still to come.

Another manifestation of automation lies within Apple's Siri, a virtual assistant that lives in the pockets of millions. Through voice commands, Siri schedules appointments, sends messages, and even controls smart home devices. This interface between human and machine epitomizes the convenience afforded by automation technology with an ever-present assistant, ready to respond to a myriad of commands, powered by AI that understands and processes natural language.

These examples typify the seamless integration of automation in various aspects of life, with each demonstrating the amalgamation of hardware, software, and AI to serve and enhance human experiences. While these technologies streamline tasks and decision-making, they also highlight the delicate balance required to maintain control, security, and user trust is a reminder that with great power comes great responsibility in stewardship and development.

Picture a morning routine subtly transformed by the intelligence of virtual assistants. A simple "Good morning" to your device can trigger a sequence of events: lights gently brighten, news and weather updates stream seamlessly through speakers, and the coffee machine stirs to life, all orchestrated by a compact hub that interprets and executes your commands with almost imperceptible effort. The virtual assistant, an emblem of modern automation, not only responds to inquiries but anticipates needs based on past interactions, blurring the lines between reactive tool and proactive aide.

Then there's the interface of the smart home environment,

responding to a tap or swipe on a smartphone screen. Whether setting the ideal temperature or locking doors remotely, these systems afford a level of control and convenience once the domain of science fiction. Yet, they are not without their intricacies. Each command sent via user interface travels a path of communication protocols to reach and activate the connected device, ensuring that human intent is translated into digital action.

These narratives of interaction with automated technologies are becoming the norm, weaving into the fabric of everyday experience. They highlight not just the capabilities of current systems, but also the continuous refinement they undergo. While virtual assistants and smart home interfaces offer a glimpse into living spaces that respond with intuition-like acuity, they also serve as a testament to the thoughtful engineering and design necessary to bring such conveniences to life. It is here, in the dance between sophisticated technology and user experience, that one finds the heart of modern automation seamlessly integrated, constantly evolving, and always striving for that personal touch that makes the everyday extraordinary.

In a landscape where automation permeates the minutiae of daily life, one must ponder the subtle yet profound ways in which this integration reshapes human behavior and societal norms. The very rhythms of existence of waking, working, communicating are being recalibrated by technologies that promise seamlessness and efficiency but also engender dependency and adaptation in turn. The ubiquity of automation influences expectations, fostering a norm where immediate gratification and predictive assistance are not exceptional, but expected.

Yet, within this tapestry of technological infusion, lie threads of complexity concerning individual autonomy and agency. As machines learn to anticipate needs and execute tasks, questions emerge around the preservation of human decision-making and the value placed on skills once deemed essential. This redefined norm challenges and yet also broadens human roles within professional and personal spheres.

The omnipresence of automation cultivates a society where the routine is reimagined, capabilities are extended, and where the definition of need expands to include the digital assistants and automated conveniences that were once luxuries. However, this new norm carries the dual responsibility of ensuring that such technology serves inclusively, bridging rather than widening divides, and reinforcing the collective good. In navigating this evolving realm, one finds an opportunity not just to embrace technological progress but to thoughtfully shape the integration of automation in a way that enhances rather than diminishes the richness of the human experience.

Automation in the fabric of everyday life has transitioned from a web of complexities to a seamless garment worn with unthinking ease. Consumer automation, once a front line of high technology, has diffused into the backdrop of our day-to-day affairs, an invisible hand that guides and facilitates our routines with ever-increasing sophistication. From the minutiae of household chores managed by smart appliances, to the grander scale of mobility assisted by AI-driven transportation, the reach of automation spans both the mundane and the exceptional. It has reshaped our habitats, our way of interacting with technology, and indeed, the very cadence of life itself.

Looking to the horizon, a confluence of advancements heralds an era where the breadth and depth of automated services will likely expand further. Interconnectivity, machine learning, and the internet of things converge to conceive systems with an ever-greater capacity to learn, adapt, and anticipate human needs. The trend towards a more automated existence is not merely an extension of what devices can do; it is, more broadly, an evolving expression of how people choose to live, work, and flourish in symbiosis with machine intelligence.

As this chapter of interaction with automation concludes, it is the thoughtful integration of these systems that will carve the path ahead. An informed engagement with the capabilities and potential of automation enables society to harness these tools for collective benefit and personal enrichment. So, as we stand at the nexus of the automated present and the autonomous future, a moment's reflection on the journey thus far can empower one to approach what comes next not just with anticipation, but with the wisdom to steer the course toward the most humane and empowering vista.

ETHICAL AND SOCIAL CONSIDERATIONS

In the world of technology, automation stands out as a powerful force shaping how work is done, goods are produced, and services are delivered. It is more than a set of technologies; it is a pivot around which many industries turn, affecting jobs, economies, and communities. The rapid growth of automated systems has thrown up several ethical and social issues that are both subtle and significant. These issues often reflect the values that societies hold and challenge them at the same time. As systems become smarter and more capable, the line between machine functions and human responsibilities grows fainter. This evolution asks us to reconsider what machines should do and what should remain in human hands. It is not just about efficiency or business outcomes; it is about the kind of future society we envision and the roles we, as individuals, have within it. Automation is not an abstract concept; it is present in the applications we use, in the cars we drive, and even in the way we shop or watch movies. Each interaction with a machine that 'thinks' and 'acts' has implications that ripple through labor markets, legal systems, and personal lives. Thus, it is crucial to analyze the layers involved, to understand what is at stake for everyone impacted--workers, business leaders, consumers, and citizens. It is a conversation that speaks to our time, defining many aspects of the human experience in the 21st century.

Automation's journey began in the late 18th century with the first machines that transformed the textile industry. This marked the onset of the Industrial Revolution. Factories started using steam-powered devices and later electrical equipment which increased production but also raised ethical questions regarding labor conditions and employment. By the 20th century, the advent of the assembly line, introduced by Henry Ford in his automobile factories, revolutionized manufacturing. This significant change increased efficiency but also led to repetitive, monotonous jobs that sparked debates about workers' mental health and overall well-being.

The mid-20th century bore witness to the next wave of change when digital computers entered the workspace. Automation started to handle not just the physical labor but also began altering the nature of clerical work. This shift brought about concerns for job security among skilled office workers and led to discussions on re-training and job transitioning strategies. Fast forwarding to the current times, artificial intelligence and robotics are the frontiers of automation. These technologies assist, and sometimes entirely replace, human decision-making and physical tasks. This progress has ignited ethical discussions on data privacy, bias in AI algorithms, and the extent to which machines should make decisions about human lives.

One notable incident that pivoted public opinion and policy was the Cambridge Analytica scandal. This event highlighted the misuse of personal data for political advertising and resulted in a call for stricter data protection laws, resulting in regulations like the General Data Protection Regulation (GDPR) in the European Union. Another turning point has been the widespread acknowledgement that AI can replicate societal biases if the data or algorithms are flawed, prompting technology companies to institute ethics boards and guidelines for responsible AI development.

Throughout these stages of automation's history, public

opinion and policy making have been shaped by the push and pull between technological advancement and ethical considerations. Each stage brought about challenges that not only advanced technological innovations but also invoked broader discussions on the societal values we hold dear. This narrative is a testament not to fear of change but to the ongoing dialogue and adjustments society makes in the face of new technology.

When considering the wide-ranging impact of automation, it is crucial to recognize the diverse group of stakeholders involved. Factory workers, for example, directly face the potential of job loss or significant changes to their roles as machines and robots take on repetitive tasks with greater efficiency. These individuals often express concerns about job security and the need for new skills training. On the other end of the spectrum are software engineers who design and build automated systems. While these professionals enjoy increased demand for their expertise, they also grapple with ethical responsibilities around the consequences of their designs on employment and society.

Business owners and managers see automation as an opportunity to cut costs and improve product consistency, yet they must contend with the human element of workforce management and the responsibility to support displaced employees. Consumers benefit from the lower prices and increased convenience afforded by automation but may show apprehension about the erosion of personal service and data privacy.

Policy-makers and regulators are tasked with balancing the economic benefits of innovation with the protection of workers' rights and the long-term societal implications. Ethicists and academics contribute to the dialogue by analyzing the effects of these technologies and by raising fundamental questions about the inherent value of human labor. They explore what a society should do to ensure ethical practices in the face of relentless progress.

These perspectives on ethical issues associated with automation form a complex web of interdependent views and interests. Understanding this landscape requires a careful analysis without oversimplification, acknowledging that the technology shaping tomorrow's workforce demands responsible governance today. This understanding is not just about accommodating new trends but ensuring that progress reflects the ethical values and societal norms that define the kind of future society aspires to create. Each stakeholder plays a role in steering the conversation and actions that will shape this outcome.

Job displacement due to automation is an issue of significant concern. A study by Martin Ford, author of "The Rise of the Robots," indicates that automation threatens to replace a large portion of the workforce, segmenting roles that are replaced entirely and those that are partially affected. Figures from his research suggest that job loss is not spread evenly across sectors or regions. While it is difficult to predict exact numbers, it is evident from historical data that roles involving routine, repetitive tasks are at the highest risk. For instance, the manufacturing sector saw a decline of about 5.6 million jobs in the United States between 2000 and 2010, primarily attributed to automation and technology improvements.

In parallel, biases in algorithms pose a silent but equally serious issue. Studies by Joy Buolamwini have found notable biases in facial recognition software, with algorithms less accurate at identifying female and darker-skinned faces. Such biases stem from the underlying data sets used to train these systems, often reflecting historical imbalances. These inaccuracies have real-world effects, such as wrongful accusations and discrimination. Cathy O'Neil's work in "Weapons of Math Destruction" highlights how algorithms used for credit scoring or hiring can perpetuate economic stratification, unfairly disadvantaging certain demographics.

Economic stratification itself becomes more pronounced with automation's rise. Thomas Piketty's research has underlined the expanding wealth gaps as high-income individuals and large corporations can invest in and benefit from automation technologies, whereas lower-income workers may face job scarcity and wage pressure. Automation can, therefore, amplify existing inequalities unless proactive measures are taken.

Contemplating these issues together reveals a landscape where the rapid evolution of automation technology intersects starkly with human economics and societal structure. They serve as a call to action for equitable and conscience-driven advancement in technology design and policy development, ensuring the future shaped by automation is inclusive and just for all members of society.

Automation has fundamentally altered many industries and, consequently, the job market. To analyze its impact on job displacement, researchers first embark on data collection. This process involves identifying roles that are most susceptible to being automated. Jobs with repetitive and predictable tasks, such as assembly line work, are typically at higher risk. Researchers often gather data through surveys or by tapping into existing employment databases, collecting details about job titles, descriptions, and associated tasks.

Metrics used to gauge displacement include the number of job vacancies, the rate of layoffs, and changes in job postings that contain keywords related to automation and technology. Statistical models, like regression analysis, are implemented to correlate the level of automation within industries with employment figures over time. These models factor in complex variables such as regional economic policies, workforce educational attainment, and industry-specific trends. This analysis extends beyond a mere headcount to consider wage stagnation and job quality.

Considering geographic and sectoral variances, the automotive industry in a technologically advanced region might face different impacts compared to a textile industry in an area with less penetration of automation technologies. These disparities arise from factors such as local economic development strategies, the supply of skilled labor, and the strength of the relevant unions.

In facial recognition technology, the data set forms the foundation upon which the algorithm is built. Training involves feeding the system a vast array of facial images tagged with identifiers like age, gender, and ethnicity. However, if the data set includes more images of one demographic group over another, the system may become less accurate for underrepresented groups. This bias manifests in higher error rates when attempting to identify individuals from these groups, leading to potential discrimination or false identifications.

Economic stratification due to automation stems from differential access to the capital required to invest in and implement such technologies. Those with more capital, such as corporations and affluent individuals, can boost productivity and profits, while those without cannot. This dynamic may exacerbate income inequality, extending the gap between high- and low-income earners. Economic models explain this through the concept of capital replacing labor ('capital-labour substitution'), where machinery takes on tasks previously performed by humans. This substitution often favors those with advanced skills ('skill-biased technological change'), increasing their value and earning potential.

A pseudo-prompt for an AI-based employment impact assessment system might read: 'Input historical job market data and automation technology adoption rates by sector. Predict job market trends over the next decade for the automotive sector.' This system would need to incorporate variables such as regional economic conditions, skill levels of the current workforce, rates of technology adoption, and data on historical job market elasticity.

Unraveling the web of factors contributing to job displacement and economic inequality helps in understanding the larger picture of automation's influence on modern society. It also underscores the need for responsive policies that mitigate adverse effects while harnessing the benefits of technological advancement.

A range of case studies exemplifies the ethical dilemmas brought on by automation. For example, consider the deployment of automated customer service chatbots in the banking industry. Here, the ethical framework revolves around concerns of transparency and privacy. Customers might not know they are interacting with an AI, which raises questions about informed consent. Stakeholder perspectives vary: customers seek efficient service while expecting the privacy of their data, whereas banks focus on reducing costs and increasing service availability. Society at large may experience the broader implications in the workforce due to reduced customer service positions.

Another case is the use of robotic process automation (RPA) in the healthcare sector for administrative tasks. Ethical frameworks guiding this scenario may include the principles of beneficence and nonmaleficence, as the automation should ideally improve care quality without causing harm, such as job losses for administrative staff. Differing stakeholders comprise healthcare providers aiming for operational efficiency, patients expecting improved healthcare delivery, and administrative workers concerned about their job security.

Finally, consider autonomous vehicles (AVs) and their fatal accidents. The ethical framework here concerns the algorithmic decision-making in life-threatening situations, often referenced as the 'trolley problem.' Auto manufacturers, as stakeholders, strive for a balance between public safety and technological progress. The public's perspective entails a mix of safety concerns, the thrill of innovation, and fears about the loss of driving-related jobs. Societally, these cases underscore the necessity for regulatory frameworks guiding the safety standards of AVs.

Each case zeroes in on specific ethical dilemmas, points at the diverse stakeholder perspectives, and reveals the broader societal repercussions of the march towards increased automation. The significance of these technicalities can be understood better when related back to the larger concepts of trust, communal welfare, and the fragile balance between innovation and its human-centered consequences.

Let's break down some examples of how Ethics would work

in current day automation:

Let's list some steps in how this would happen.

Step 1: Ethical Principles in Financial Chatbots

In the finance sector, chatbots programmed to handle customer queries must adhere to principles like transparency, which dictates that users should be aware they are interacting with a machine. For consent, users must actively agree to data collection, and privacy policies should protect personal financial information. To design ethical chatbots, developers encode these principles into every chat interaction, informing users of the chatbot's AI nature and requesting consent before proceeding with personalized assistance.

Step 2: Data Processing and Safeguards

Financial chatbots typically process data such as transaction history and account details to provide relevant assistance. This processing requires strict data handling protocols to ensure user data privacy. Encryption, anonymization, and security features like multi-factor authentication are safeguards used to secure personal data. Regular audits and compliance checks are also performed to maintain ethical use standards.

Step 3: Healthcare RPA Implementation and Monitoring

Robotic Process Automation (RPA) in healthcare starts with identifying administrative processes suitable for automation, such as appointment scheduling or claim processing. These tasks should not detract from patient care quality or staff well-being. Engagement with staff is essential to facilitate a smooth transition to new automated routines. To monitor the impacts, healthcare providers set performance metrics for service quality and conduct regular assessments to detect any detrimental effects on employment.

Step 4: Ethical Programming of Autonomous Vehicle Algorithms

For autonomous vehicles (AV), the decision-making algorithms are highly complex, responsible for real-time responses to dynamic road situations. In potentially dangerous scenarios, these algorithms follow ethical guidelines promulgated by industry standards, such as minimizing harm. Developers simulate a multitude of traffic scenarios and pre-program appropriate vehicle reactions, often adopting a conservative approach that errs on the side of caution.

Step 5: Ethical Guidelines and Developer Responsibility

AV developers must comply with ethical guidelines that prioritize safety and public welfare. They engage in ongoing discourse with ethicists, policymakers, and the public to navigate the challenges of algorithmic ethics in life-threatening situations. Transparency in these processes and the reasoning behind certain decisions is crucial in garnering public trust.

In each step, the significance of ethical considerations in the design and application of automated systems is evident. Balancing technological capabilities with ethical safeguards is not just about meeting legal requirements but about ensuring that innovation progresses with the welfare of individuals and society firmly at its core.

Current policies and regulations regarding automation are diverse and vary by country and industry. In general, these measures aim to ensure that automation benefits both businesses and workers, while minimizing potential harms. For example, certain labor laws have been adjusted to account for the new ways in which work is performed and overseen when automation is involved. In terms of regulatory approaches, agencies might impose standards to guarantee the safety and reliability of automated systems, particularly those involved in transport and healthcare.

Evaluating the effectiveness of these strategies reveals a mixed picture. In some cases, regulations have struggled to keep pace with the rapid development of technology. This lag can lead to gaps in oversight and protection for both workers and consumers. Conversely, some policies have successfully steered the development of automation towards more ethical practices, such as those ensuring transparency in AI decision-making processes.

Thought leaders and policymakers have proposed several forward-thinking solutions to address these issues. These include a 'robot tax' to offset the social costs of displaced workers, and the development of universal basic income schemes to support individuals as the job market evolves. Another suggestion is to incentivize the re-skilling of workers, preparing them for the new roles created by automation. There is also a push for 'explainable AI' that allows users to understand how automated decisions are made, which could foster greater trust in the technology.

All these proposals center on a proactive approach to the challenges of automation. They represent concerted efforts to predict future shifts in the economy and workforce, and to prepare society for these changes. Such strategies underline the importance of balancing innovation with ethical considerations and societal well-being.

Ethical guidelines and professional standards in automation are essential frameworks that dictate responsible practices.

These standards originate from a mix of professional ethics, legal requirements, and societal norms. Organizations like the Institute of Electrical and Electronics Engineers (IEEE) and the Association for Computing Machinery (ACM) set forth guidelines that inform professionals in the field. For example, the IEEE's Ethically Aligned Design and the ACM's Code of Ethics and Professional Conduct both outline principles of human rights, transparency, accountability, and privacy protection.

In practical terms, these guidelines mean that systems must be developed to perform reliably without infringing on individuals' rights or causing unintended harm. For instance, any application of automated facial recognition technology in public surveillance should clearly outline the measures taken to prevent the misuse of data, uphold data subjects' privacy rights, and rectify any errors in identification without delay.

To apply these guidelines, developers and engineers undergo training on ethical decision-making and legal compliance. Companies may establish review boards to evaluate whether proposed systems meet ethical thresholds before deployment. Additionally, third-party audits can provide an independent assessment of compliance with ethical standards.

In contention enforcement, penalties for non-compliance with professional standards vary. They may range from reputational damage and loss of professional accreditation to legal actions and fines imposed by regulatory authorities. In high-stakes scenarios, such as the deployment of autonomous vehicles or medical diagnostics tools, stringent testing protocols are in place to verify that the systems operate within the defined ethical parameters.

These ethical guidelines and professional standards serve as the foundation for trust in automation technology. By adhering to these stipulated norms, professionals and organizations commit to steering the development of automation towards outcomes that safeguard human dignity and societal welfare.

The formation of ethical standards within organizations like the IEEE and ACM entails systematic steps, starting with the identification of need. These needs often arise from new technological capabilities that present unforeseen consequences. Next, a diverse panel of experts conducts research, engages in debates, and reviews case studies that illustrate potential ethical pitfalls. They gather varied input from stakeholders, including industry professionals, academics, legal professionals, and the public. The goal is to achieve a balance that considers innovation potential, public interest, and individual rights.

After drafting the guidelines, a broader consultation process ensures that the guidelines are practical and comprehensive. The finalized standards are then published and distributed to the professional community. Education on these standards is often integrated into certification programs and ongoing professional development trains professionals ranging from software developers to system engineers.

In the assessment of automation projects for ethical alignment, each stage of development is analyzed against the guidelines. Specific job roles include an ethics officer, who ensures that the design phase upholds the stipulated ethical principles and a legal compliance manager, who oversees the implementation phase's adherence to both ethical and legal requirements. These professionals use checklists and decision trees to examine the nuances of each project scenario.

When ethical breaches occur, an internal review by an ethics committee within the company can escalate, if warranted, to an external investigative body, which can impose sanctions. These escalate from warnings and mandatory re-training to professional disbarment or legal action, depending on the severity of the breach.

An example of a pseudo prompt for an ethics training session could be: 'Given a set of user data management scenarios, identify potential breaches of the ACM Code of Ethics related to user consent and data privacy.' The trainee would systematically evaluate each scenario against established ethical guidelines, deciding the most ethical course of action.

This detailed account of ethical standards creation and implementation illustrates the importance of structured processes in maintaining societal trust as automation becomes increasingly prevalent in diverse sectors. Through adherence to these guiding principles, professionals ensure that the development and deployment of automated systems align with society's broader goals and respect individual rights.

According to recent studies and analyses by experts in technology and economics, the trajectory of automation is paving the way for a transformative future. Data indicates that by 2030, intelligent automation could contribute up to $15 trillion to the global economy. This financial impact underscores the speed at which machine learning, artificial intelligence, and robotics are being integrated into industries ranging from manufacturing and transportation to healthcare and finance.

As automation permeates these sectors, the ethical

challenges it presents will become more intricately woven into the fabric of daily life. Privacy concerns that arise from data collection used to power AI systems are likely to grow, necessitating stronger regulations and more robust cybersecurity measures. Job displacement will also remain a pressing issue. Projections suggest a significant shift in the labor market with a demand for new skills and job roles, sparking debates on education reform and workforce reskilling initiatives.

Moreover, the increased reliance on automation will heighten the stakes in discussions about algorithmic bias and accountability. With decisions that could affect millions being made by automated systems, ensuring fairness and transparency becomes paramount. Public policy, corporate accountability, and international collaboration will play crucial roles in addressing these evolving ethical concerns.

This narrative paints a picture of a future where human ingenuity, ethical foresight, and technological advancement must align to navigate a world reshaped by the relentless march of automation. It calls for proactive engagement from all corners of society to craft a landscape where the benefits of automation are realized while its ethical challenges are judiciously managed.

As this exploration of automation and its ethical implications draws to a close, one fact remains clear: ethical consideration is as integral to technological advancement as the technology itself. Throughout this chapter, the detailed insights into job displacement, bias in algorithms, and privacy concerns have not only highlighted challenges but also underscored the responsibility inherent in navigating this new terrain. It is evident that automation's march forward brings with it a profound responsibility to ensure fairness, protect individuals' rights, and prepare societies for transformative change. The dialogue on these topics requires continued, forward-looking engagement. This call to action is not limited to professionals and policymakers; every individual has a stake in this future. Your voice is critical in these conversations, helping to shape a world where automation serves as a tool for empowerment and progress, harnessed within the thoughtful bounds of ethical frameworks. Therefore, stay informed, remain curious, and contribute proactively as we together shape a future that reflects the best of human intention and moral stewardship in the age of automation.

THE ECONOMIC IMPLICATIONS OF AUTOMATION

As one surveys the economic landscape of the past century, automation emerges as a formidable force, driving momentous shifts that have redefined productivity, industry structures, and the labor force. It began with mechanization in manufacturing: assembly lines augmenting human labor, a first ripple that would grow into a wave of change. Over time, automation transcended the physical, as computers and software systems streamlined administrative processes, carving efficiency into the bedrock of businesses.

With the advent of digital automation, productivity experienced a seismic shift. Machines and algorithms capable of executing tasks at unparalleled speeds became a mainstay, allowing for outputs that burgeoned beyond the limitations of human pace and endurance. This surging productivity has reshaped entire industries, leading to burgeoning sectors such as information technology and e-commerce, while traditional fields have metamorphosed, integrating automated solutions to maintain competitive relevance.

Yet, the reach of automation extends beyond the confines of commercial ventures, entwining with the sinews of the labor force. Its narrative is twofold: while opening vistas for new skills and professions data analysts, AI specialists, and more it has also initiated a phasing out of roles that once rested solely on human shoulders. The labor force faces a crucible of change, where the adaptability and lifelong learning are not merely valued but vital.

In tracing automation's arc of influence, one uncovers a pattern of continual reinvention and a dynamic interplay between human endeavor and machine capability, cocreating a tomorrow that reflects the revolutionary yet intricate dance of progress. The understanding of automation's multifaceted impact does more than inform; it equips one with the perspective and foresight to harness this momentum, to navigate the course of economic evolution with both wisdom and anticipation.

Data from national economies and the analyses of esteemed economists converge to tell a story of automation's profound implications. In this examination, it becomes evident that automation acts as a lever on employment patterns, pushing forth the dichotomy of job displacement and job creation. For every robotic arm that streamlines production, there is a pivot in workforce demand with less need for manual assembly line workers, yet a rise in the call for skilled technicians who can oversee and maintain such systems.

This shift leads to a reallocation and transformation of the labor market, where the demand for routine manual and cognitive skills diminishes, and the demand for higher-order skills burgeots. It's a development that, while potentially increasing productivity, can also contribute to wage polarization, where high-skilled workers reap greater rewards while middle-skill roles face compressed wages, further exacerbating income inequality.

Yet on the macro scale, automation has the propensity to fuel economic growth. Through heightened productivity, it broadens the capacity of economies to expand output without proportional increases in labor input. Singular examples can be seen in the manufacturing sectors of developed nations where, despite a decrease in employment, there has often been notable growth in output, evidencing automation's contribution to economic expansion.

However, these macro-level benefits do not uniformly permeate within an economy; rather, they distribute unevenly, presenting policymakers with the challenge of harnessing automation's growth potential while mitigating its potential to widen socio-economic gaps. The interplay between automation, economic structure, and labor dynamics engenders a complex web that demands ongoing scrutiny and agile policy frameworks to ensure that advancements contribute positively to national economic narratives and, by extension, to the global financial landscape.

In a dissection of automation's economic narrative, sector-by-sector scrutiny unveils its intricate implications. Within manufacturing, automation has augmented output while trimming the workforce with a mitigation of labor costs reflected in national productivity statistics. For example, the United States' Bureau of Labor Statistics reports a significant increase in manufacturing output per hour, juxtaposed against a decrease in employment within the sector. This dichotomy underscores a change in basic assumptions where productivity gains no longer correlate directly with employment growth.

In transportation, autonomous vehicle technologies forecast a transformation of commercial fleets and public transit, promising heightened efficiency but also signaling a future drop in demand for human drivers. Conversely, the service industry faces a nuanced upheaval, with AI-driven platforms capable of scheduling and customer service functions leading to a reformation of service roles. Wage patterns here reveal a skew towards higher remuneration for tech-savvy positions, even as traditional roles encounter wage stagnation.

Empirical data sketches a dual-sided picture: a report by McKinsey Global Institute suggests that nearly half of current work activities have the potential for automation, which could equate to global economic impact ranging into trillions of dollars. On the macro scale, the wave of automation implicates GDP growth trajectories, capital investment in technology, and the global flows of trade, reshaping economies towards sectors that integrate automation more fervently.

Grasping the societal ripples of this transition, policy responses have emerged aimed at harmonizing the integration of automation. South Korea's aggressive investment in robotics, coupled with worker retraining initiatives, mirrors a pursuit to create an innovative, technologically proficient economy. In the European Union, policies around digital taxation attempt to equalize the playing field for traditional and tech-driven enterprises, all under the aegis of ensuring social equity amidst economic transformation.

Thus, the economic tapestry woven by automation is one of complex patterns, where micro-level effects percolate up to macroeconomic outcomes and back down to the fabric of societal policy and structure. A measured appreciation of these dynamics enables both a rooted grasp on the current state and an insightful gaze towards the ramifications that automation may herald for the economic landscapes of tomorrow.

The tale of automation's impact is replete with narratives of duality, where technological advancement is both a blessing and a cross to bear. In the manufacturing realm, case studies highlight a surge in productivity catalyzed by robotic automation. Factories have become paragons of efficiency as robots perform tasks with unwavering precision and speed with a boon for output and competitive edge. For instance, take a car manufacturing plant, where robotic arms engage in welding and assembling parts, undertaking tasks around the clock without fatigue, leading to a streamlined production line that scales heights previously beyond human capability.

However, parallel to these gains run stories of displacement in sectors where automation plays a distinctly different role. Retail, for example, faces the proliferation of self-service kiosks and checkout systems, tools that, while optimizing customer experience and operational efficiency, also reshape the workforce. These systems reduce the need for cashiers, translating into job losses and a shift towards roles that design, program, and maintain automated systems. As such, where employment prospects dim in certain sectors, they brighten in the tech-centric terrains.

This dichotomy paints a portrait of automation where the multifarious effects necessitate a closer examination beyond surface-level impacts. The nuances of these shifts must be acknowledged and comprehensively understood with an initiative that serves not only to grasp the current state of affairs but also to empower stakeholders to mitigate the negative repercussions while harnessing the positive forces driving this change. It is in this understanding that society can fully appreciate the dualistic nature of automation, reflecting on both its capacity to foster innovation and productivity and its potential to recalibrate the job market.

As automation weaves its intricate patterns through the labor market, a keen observation reveals a metamorphosis in the realm of employment. Job roles once static now evolve; skills that garnered demand adapt under technology's sway. Take, for example, the bank teller's position, which, in the wake of automated teller machines and online banking platforms, transitions from cash transaction handling to customer service and financial advisory with a nuanced shift in responsibilities driven by the prefatory steps of automation.

Moreover, this advent of sophisticated technology births entirely new categories of employment. The data analyst, a profession scarcely conceivable in the pre-digital era, emerges out of the need to filter, interpret, and glean insights from the deluge of data that automation systems produce. In parallel, roles such as AI ethicists and automation strategists begin to populate the job market, reflecting the growing intricacies associated with aligning machine efficiency with human values and strategic goals.

To comprehend the depth and breadth of such transformation, one must dissect the components and machines that model patterns replace rote procedure; algorithms that parse customer behavior inform marketing strategies and product development. Each role that automation subsumes or transforms directs human capital towards tasks that necessitate critical thinking, creativity, and interpersonal skills which are the quintessentially human facets that machines have yet to master.

This evolution of the labor market, from binary simplicity to multifaceted complexity, bears witness to the potential of humans and machines in concert. It guides the observant through a labor landscape that is not diminishing but is diversifying, opening vistas of opportunity for those who navigate the change with awareness and agility. It is within this detailed understanding of labor market dynamics that one finds the keys to not just surviving but thriving in the age of automation.

Embarking on a comprehensive study requires delving into the labyrinth of automation's influence on employment across pivotal industries. In finance, the advent of high-frequency trading algorithms and automated risk assessment tools marks a before-and-after scenario, where job roles shift from traditional stock trading to data-centric financial analysis. Examination of labor statistics reveals a decline in conventional finance positions, countered by a burgeoning demand for quantitative analysts and compliance specialists, reflecting the sector's shift to a technology-driven ecosystem.

The manufacturing industry offers a stark visualization of this transition, with robotics and automated assembly lines mirroring the reduction in manual labor roles. Economic records indicate an uptick in productivity concurrent with a tapering of manufacturing jobs, although wages for remaining roles show an upward trend, suggesting an increase in the value of enhanced technical skill sets.

Healthcare, transformed by automation in diagnostics, patient data management, and even surgery, illustrates a pivot towards tech-enabled care. The growth of medical technology roles like biomedical engineers, informatics specialists, and telemedicine coordinators portrays an industry adapting to an automation-enhanced future.

In the realm of technology itself, automation is a recursive catalyst, sparking the creation of job roles that, in turn, propel further automation. Software developers for AI applications, robotics engineers, and user experience designers for automated systems stand as testaments to the burgeoning employment landscape.

Synthesizing this data paints a picture of labor markets in flux and a dynamic tableau where the augmentation of human roles is as significant as the displacement automation may cause. This study would propose a projection model, accounting for trends such as the intensification of AI and continued robotics integration, hypothesizing potential job saturation points and emerging sectors primed for growth.

Policies that foster workforce agility, such as targeted education initiatives and upskilling programs, emerge as macro-level recommendations. On an individual scale, the development of interdisciplinary skill sets aligns with a labor market that increasingly values adaptability and tech literacy. By pivoting the lens of analysis from what jobs will be lost to what jobs will emerge and how to prepare for them, this study reframes the narrative of automation in the labor market from one of challenge to one of opportunity. The final insight draws from the branches of data to the root conclusion: a future-ready workforce hinges on understanding these intricate economic patterns and proactively sowing the seeds of adaptation and growth.

Regional responses to the surge of automation reflect a tapestry of strategies, each woven from the unique economic fibers and social fabrics of their respective geographies. In Asia, for instance, countries like South Korea and Japan, known for their robust manufacturing sectors, bolster investments in robotics, aiming to amplify productivity while also addressing shrinking labor pools due to aging populations. Such strategic investments underscore a commitment to maintain industrial competitiveness, yet they carry an undercurrent of workforce implications that require careful navigation.

European governance, characteristically thoughtful of worker welfare, tackles automation by advocating for policies that balance technological progress with social interests. For example, discussions within the European Union include considerations of "robot taxes" to fund social welfare systems and an acknowledgement of the potential for job displacement and a bid to ensure that the benefits of automation extend across the socio-economic spectrum.

Across the Atlantic, the United States presents a mosaic approach, with initiatives varying at the federal, state, and local levels. While some municipalities embrace automation to rejuvenate industries and attract businesses, others deploy workforce development programs targeting sectors susceptible to automation. Training and education, in concert with private sector partnerships, form the crux of efforts to equip workers with the tools to transition into the tech-infused economy of the future.

The prevailing thread among these varied regional tactics is the recognition that automation, while inexorable in its march, must be guided with foresight and aligned with policies designed to maximize its potential while safeguarding societal well-being. It is within this framework that regions and governing bodies map out pathways through the labyrinth of automation's advance and a journey that requires the clarity of vision and the precision of policies to ensure that its benefits are both realized and shared.

In the fertile grounds of the financial sector, automation has germinated a revolution, from the roots of traditional practices to the fruits of algorithmic trading and fintech innovations. Algorithmic trading harnesses complex computational formulas to execute trades at volumes and speeds beyond human capacity. Here, algorithms function as traders, sifting through market data in real time, identifying patterns and executing buy or sell orders based on predefined criteria with meticulous precision and unemotional calculation.

Fintech, or financial technology, is the broader canopy under which these advancements proliferate. It encompasses a sapling of mobile banking, where machine learning algorithms personalize banking experiences, predict financial needs, and enhance security protocols through anomaly detection. Peer-to-peer lending platforms circumvent conventional banking altogether, pairing borrowers with lenders through automated screening processes, democratizing access to capital.

Underneath these innovations is a shared foundation: the utilization of data to amplify the efficiency and accessibility of financial services. Automated systems in finance dissect large datasets to forecast market trends and tailor services to individual user profiles, thereby recalibrating risk evaluations, streamlining transaction processes, and personalizing financial guidance.

As one extends the viewfinder to the panoramic vista of finance, automated systems emerge as pivotal in sculpting an industry that is more agile, incisive, and inclusive. Yet this transformation is not without its thorns; as the financial landscape is reshaped, so too are the responsibilities to monitor the integrity of these systems, balance privacy with personalization, and ensure the solvency of markets within an increasingly automated orchestra of economic exchange.

Algorithmic trading, an intricate mosaic of strategies executed by computers, revolutionizes the traditional market exchange approach. Let us discern the cogs of this machinery: arbitrage algorithms detect price discrepancies across markets, executing simultaneous trades to capitalize on these fleeting opportunities. For example:

```
if price_security_A_exchange_1 < price_security_A_exchange_2:
    buy security_A_exchange_1
    sell security_A_exchange_2
    profit = sell_price - buy_price
```

Trend-following algorithms, on the other hand, identify directional movements in market prices and follow these trends to execute trades. They might track moving averages to determine the momentum:

```
if current_price > moving_average_price:
    create long_position()
elif current_price < moving_average_price:
    create short_position()
```

Market-making algorithms balance buy and sell orders to

provide liquidity, capturing the spread between the bidding and asking prices:

```
for new_order in market_orders:
    if new_order is buy and < current_ask:
        set new_ask = new_order.price
    elif new_order is sell and > current_bid:
        set new_bid = new_order.price
```

This execution is predicated on data analysis. Historical patterns, real-time feeds, and predictive analytics inform the strategy, turning raw data into a roadmap for trading decisions.

Transitioning to fintech, machine learning in banking harnesses consumer data to tailor user experience and fortify security. Banks implement models that traverse through transaction history to flag fraudulent patterns, learning from user behavior to construct a profile of regular activity. When a transaction deviates starkly from this profile, the model flags it for review:

```
def transaction_review(transaction):
    if transaction not in typical_user_behavior:
        flag for security_review()
```

Through this method, mobile banking becomes not just smarter but safer. Such technological tapestry paints a sector in transformation, where financial operations harmonize with algorithmic precision, inducing a leap from manual analysis to data-driven decision-making paradigms. Engrained in this evolution is a narrative of efficiency, security, and, most critically, an ever-deepening interweave between human financial intellect and the potent capabilities of automated systems.

In the spectrum of policy discourse, governments and think tanks are scrutinizing a variety of strategies to buffer the tectonic shifts induced by automation. One such approach is the taxation of automated systems with a proposal aimed at recalibrating the fiscal landscape to account for the reduced income tax that follows from displaced human labor. Proponents argue that revenue derived from such taxes could bolster social safety nets and fund public services, yet detractors worry about stifling innovation or incentivizing companies to relocate to more tax-friendly areas.

Simultaneously, the concept of a universal basic income (UBI) is gaining traction as a means to decouple livelihoods from traditional employment amidst the automation upheaval. The premise here is simple: provide all citizens with a no-strings-attached monetary allowance sufficient for living, thereby ensuring economic stability as the job market morphs. Trials of UBI exhibit mixed outcomes, highlighting the intricacies of its implementation of how it is funded, its impact on work incentives, and its effect on social cohesion and individual well-being are points of lively debate.

These policy considerations unfold against a backdrop of

technological advancement where the ethos is to preemptively address the socioeconomic effects of automation. The intention is clear with designing a policy framework that not only navigates the current implications of automation but also anticipates its future trajectory, ensuring economic resilience and social welfare in the face of relentless innovation. It is in the confluence of foresighted policy-making and a deep understanding of automation's potential that societies may find sustainable pathways through the economic renaissance heralded by this new age of machines.

This chapter has journeyed through the intricate landscape where automation interfaces with the sinews of contemporary economics. The findings unearth a multifaceted truth: automation, in its relentless march, has become a bedrock of productivity and a catalyst for industry evolution. Leaning into the sweeping changes, it redraws the contours of labor demands, nudges GDP growth, and reshapes the skills that fuel economic engines. Yet, these advancements are not without their shadows, casting the risk of obsolescence on certain sectors and engendering new challenges for workforce adaptation.

In the weave of this narrative, it becomes clear that automation's influence extends far beyond the ledger and assembly line, touching on the profound interplay of equity, efficiency, and employment. As it accelerates economies, it calls into question the sustainability of traditional economic models and the social contracts upon which they rest. The implications for future socio-economic structures are considerable; they hint at a need for flexibility in policy, education, and vocational training to equip societies for an automated future.

A finer appreciation of the nuances in automation's tale reveals the undercurrents that may define the socio-economic reality of tomorrow. The vision of future structures reflects not a static acceptance of automation but an active engagement with its ripple effects, encouraging policies that foster an economy resilient in the face of technological tides. This understanding of automation in the context of economics does more than elucidate; it empowers individuals, businesses, and governments to chart purposeful courses through the complex yet promising terrain ahead.

THE FUTURE IS AUTOMATED

The story of automation begins in the shadowy factories of the Industrial Revolution, where the first machines revolutionized the way people worked and lived. Fast forward to today, and the landscape is alive with the buzz of artificial intelligence (AI), robotics, and sophisticated algorithms that make decisions, drive cars, and even create art. This journey from steam-powered looms to intelligent systems capable of learning and adapting is a testament to human ingenuity. Looking ahead, technology is poised to blend even more seamlessly with daily life, promising not only to augment human capabilities but also to reshape economies and redefine societal norms. As these smart systems grow in complexity and ability, they evoke a sense of wonder about the future's potential for a harmonious partnership with machines. The vision of tomorrow reflects not a world overridden by automation but one enriched by it, where technology serves to elevate the human experience. It is a narrative not of replacement but of enhancement, where the synergy between man and machine unlocks untapped potential and heralds an era of unparalleled progress.

Recent trends in AI development and automation reveal a rapid expansion of capabilities and applications. For instance, advancements in machine learning have led to systems that can learn more efficiently from smaller data sets, a shift that enhances AI's adaptability and utility. In robotics, machines are gaining dexterity and sensitivity, allowing them to perform tasks that were once thought to exclusively require a human touch. Projections from scholars indicate that, in the coming years, AIs could surpass human performance not only in structured environments but also in more complex tasks like dynamic decision-making and creative endeavors.

These technologies' proliferation is set to change how society operates, with possible shifts in employment patterns, healthcare accessibility, and even governance. Reports suggest a reconfiguration of job markets, urging an increase in STEM education and re-skilling efforts to prepare workers for a digitized economy. Meanwhile, ethical discussions intensify over the deployment of AI, calling for rigorous oversight to ensure fairness, accountability, and respect for privacy.

As such, the insight gained from scholarly predictions paints a picture of a future where AI's role is increasingly pivotal, with the potential to bring about significant societal transformation. The discussion ensures the reader gains a comprehensive understanding of AI and automation's trajectory, poised on the brink of reshaping modern life's very fabric.

In the realm of artificial intelligence, significant breakthroughs have been made that augment machine learning. These include neural networks that mimic human brain function to increase learning efficiency and generative adversarial networks (GANs) that pit two AI systems against each other to improve data output. Advances in transfer learning allow AIs to apply knowledge learned from one task to accomplish another, drastically reducing the time required for training on new tasks.

The rise of autonomous systems such as self-driving cars and drones incorporates complex sensor arrays and decision-making algorithms that allow them to navigate and interact safely within their environment. These vehicles analyze real-time data, make quick decisions to avoid obstacles, and learn from each journey to improve future performance.

Cognitive architectures create systems that can engage in human-like reasoning. For example, IBM's Project Debater can construct persuasive arguments on a wide range of topics, engaging in live debates with humans. These breakthroughs have clear, practical applications, from precision farming using autonomous drones that monitor and treat crops, to advanced assistance systems that improve accessibility for individuals with disabilities by interpreting natural language and responding to spoken commands.

Each of these advancements in AI underscores the capability of machines to handle increasingly complex tasks, opening doors to enhancements across various sectors, including healthcare, agriculture, and transportation. This detailed analysis emphasizes the revolutionary impact these technologies have on both industry practices and daily human activities.

Neural Network Function and Backpropagation:
Neural networks consist of layers of interconnected nodes or 'neurons' that process input data to generate output relevant to specific tasks, like image or speech recognition. These layers include an input layer, one or more hidden layers, and an output layer. During the forward pass, data moves through these layers, and each neuron assigns weights to its inputs, which are adjusted by biases. The neuron's output is then computed through an activation function that determines its level of 'activation' or influence on the next layer.

Backpropagation is an algorithm for iteratively updating the weights and biases in a neural network. It starts by calculating the error at the output layer - the difference between the predicted result and the actual outcome. The process involves moving backward through the network (thus 'backpropagation'), calculating gradients of the error with respect to the neuron weights, known as the 'gradient descent.' Using these gradients, the algorithm adjusts the weights to minimize the error, improving the model's predictions over rounds of training.

Let's break down some of the technologies we mentioned:

Generative Adversarial Networks (GANs):
GANs involve two neural networks: a generator and a discriminator. The generator creates new, synthetic instances of data, while the discriminator evaluates them against real data sets. The interaction can be described simply in pseudo-code as follows:

```
generator = build_generator_network()
discriminator = build_discriminator_network()
for each epoch in training_cycles:
    fake_data = generator(input_random_noise)
    real_data = get_batch_from_real_dataset()
    if discriminator(real_data) < discriminator(fake_data):
        update generator weights to improve fake data realism
    else:
        update discriminator weights to improve fake vs. real distinction
```

Transfer Learning:
Transfer learning enables a model developed for one task to

apply its learned features, like edge detection in images, to a new but related task, such as diagnosing medical conditions from scans. This is akin to a person using knowledge from one area (like mathematics) to solve problems in another (like physics).

Example transfer learning steps:
1. Begin with a model trained on a vast image dataset.
2. Remove the last output layer of the model, replacing it with one tailored to the new medical diagnosis task.
3. Use a smaller, specialized dataset of medical images to fine-tune the model, training only the new layers.
4. Test the model on unseen medical data to validate its diagnostic accuracy.

Algorithms in Autonomous Systems:
Algorithms within autonomous systems digest sensor inputs to navigate environments. Here's a simplified pseudo-prompt for an autonomous vehicle's decision-making algorithm:

```
sensor_data = collect_lidar_camera_radar_data()
current_location = determine_vehicle_location(sensor_data)
desired_location = get_destination_coordinates()
obstacles = identify_obstacles(sensor_data)
optimal_path = plan_route(current_location, desired_location, obstacles)
while vehicle_not_at_destination(current_location, desired_location):
    actuate_controls(optimal_path)
    sensor_data = collect_lidar_camera_radar_data()
    update optimal_path if necessary
```

Cognitive Architectures like Project Debater:

Cognitive architectures allow AI systems to mimic aspects of human thought. Project Debater might use NLP (Natural Language Processing) to parse and understand language, knowledge representation to store and recall information, and machine learning to refine its argumentation techniques. The system could include:

1. An NLP parser that breaks down sentences into semantic structures.

2. A database that holds factual information and common arguments on various topics.

3. An argumentative engine that selects and structures arguments based on the input query and context.

4. A feedback loop where the system learns from engagements, optimizing for more compelling argument construction.

In detailing these AI components, mechanisms, and architectures, a clear, step-by-step approach is employed that aids understandability. By breaking down the complex processes into their fundamental parts, the reader can appreciate the intricacies of each technique and the broader impact on technology's capabilities.

Automation and AI have significantly transformed industries such as manufacturing and healthcare. In manufacturing, case studies reveal the shift from manual assembly lines to automated systems that improve precision and efficiency. A prime example is the automotive industry, where robots execute tasks ranging from welding to intricate parts assembly. This has resulted in higher productivity, though it also necessitates a rethinking of workforce skills and job roles.

In healthcare, AI applications are advancing diagnostic

accuracy and personalizing patient care. For example, AI algorithms process medical imaging faster and often more accurately than human radiologists, leading to earlier and more precise diagnoses. These technical advances have broad implications, including the shift towards preventive medicine and the need for new regulatory practices to ensure patient safety and privacy.

Key public figures, including industry leaders and policymakers, play pivotal roles in steering these advancements. Elon Musk's initiatives in automating manufacturing processes through his companies influence both the rate of adoption of these technologies and the public conversation around them. Similarly, healthcare innovators like Fei-Fei Li advocate for AI systems that augment medical professionals' work, not replace them, guiding the industry towards augmentation rather than automation. The social shifts from these changes are profound, transforming job markets, necessitating new education and training programs, and raising ethical debates about the balance between efficiency and employment.

Ethical considerations in the advancing field of automation and artificial intelligence are multifaceted and critical. Privacy concerns emerge as AI systems process vast amounts of personal data to deliver tailored services or insights. This raises the need for stringent data protection measures, as exemplified by the General Data Protection Regulation (GDPR) in the European Union, which sets a precedent for global data privacy standards.

Job displacement is another ethical challenge, as the integration of AI into industries can alter employment landscapes. Thought leaders like Andrew Yang propose solutions such as Universal Basic Income to alleviate the potential negative effects on workers, igniting a debate on the social safety nets required in an automated future.

Regarding decision-making algorithms, issues of transparency and accountability come to the forefront. The increasing role of these algorithms in various sectors — from finance to criminal justice — spotlights the necessity for oversight to ensure decisions are fair and non-discriminatory. Initiatives like the AI Now Institute at New York University work to understand AI's social implications, advocating for public discourse and the development of checks and balances to govern the deployment of intelligent systems.

Collectively, these discussions form a narrative in which both the potential and the limitations of technology must be acknowledged. The conversation continues, as does the need for a proactive approach to integrate ethical considerations into technological innovation.

Artificial intelligence stands at the convergence with critical fields, significantly enhancing capabilities and expanding possibilities. In biotechnology, AI algorithms analyze complex biological data to deliver breakthroughs in genetic sequencing and drug discovery, accelerating treatment personalization for diseases like cancer. In renewable energy, machine learning optimizes grid management, integrating variable inputs from solar and wind sources effectively and predicting energy demand patterns with high accuracy.

Space exploration, too, harnesses AI for autonomous navigation across extraterrestrial landscapes and to process vast amounts of data from space telescopes and rovers. This aids in making informed decisions about mission paths, and identifying astrobiological signs of life with minimal human oversight.

Scholarly predictions and current research suggest that this synergy will continue to grow, especially as computing power increases and algorithms become more adept at handling multidimensional data. The outlook is one of a smarter future where AI enables quantum leaps in understanding and manipulating biological systems, enhances efficiency in clean energy, and broadens the human horizon to the far reaches of space.

These integrations are not merely academic; they have practical implications, such as personalized medicine becoming more accessible, renewables gaining higher adoption rates, and space missions becoming more ambitious in scope and scale. As these technologies mature, the blending of AI with other scientific disciplines will lead to an era where the collaborative potential of these combined domains is fully realized, offering opportunities to tackle some of the world's most pressing challenges.

In biotechnology, artificial intelligence, particularly deep learning models, plays a pivotal role in genetic sequencing. These AI models process complex biological data, recognizing patterns and variations in genetic sequences that are often imperceptible to human analysis. They can predict how different genetic mutations may affect health outcomes, which in turn, informs the creation of personalized medicine treatments tailored to an individual's genetic makeup. An example is a convolutional neural network, a deep learning model particularly adept at image analysis, which identifies patterns in genetic data to detect markers associated with diseases.

Moving to renewable energy, AI systems analyze meteorological data to predict weather changes that affect energy production, especially in solar and wind power. Simultaneously, they analyze consumption trends from smart meters to predict energy demand. A typical predictive model for energy demand could proceed as follows: collect data on past energy usage, factor in future weather conditions using neural networks trained on historical data, and then produce an energy demand forecast, which informs energy supply management, ensuring both efficiency and continuity of supply.

In space exploration, AI augments the analysis of vast amounts of image data from rovers and satellites. These AI systems use a variety of image recognition algorithms to scrutinize photos of planetary surfaces, identify geological formations, analyze atmospheric data, or even detect chemical compositions from spectrographic images. The data interpreted by AI helps scientists make decisions about exploration focus areas, potentially finding indications of extraterrestrial life or valuable resources.

Each use of AI in these fields relies on its ability to synthesize and interpret vast datasets far beyond human capability, offering novel approaches to longstanding challenges. The practical applications of this advanced analysis unlock new frontiers in scientific research and day-to-day utility, demonstrating the widespread transformative power of AI.

The advance of automation is propelling forward at an unprecedented pace, carrying the potential to reshape every facet of human endeavor. It brings the promise of increased efficiency, enhanced safety, and capabilities that stretch beyond the limits of human stamina and precision. Amid this surge of technological possibility, it is critical to engage with these tools with a deep sense of responsibility. This means remaining vigilant about how automation influences employment, privacy, and social dynamics, ensuring that progress does not come at the cost of ethical compromise or widening inequality. Every individual, whether a technologist, policymaker, or citizen, holds the power to contribute to the discourse that will sculpt the ethical contours of this automated future. The narrative ahead is not just written by codes and algorithms but also by human values and decisions. Striving for a future that respects both the awe-inspiring potential of automation and the foundational principles of human society is not only an aspiration but a collective responsibility.

CONCLUSION

As we close the final chapter of 'AI Is Taking Over The World,' it is clear that the age of automation is not a distant prospect on the horizon but an unfolding reality shaping the minutiae of our daily lives. This book has chronicled the silent yet profound revolution where artificial intelligence and machine-driven systems have begun to take the helm in industries, homes, and even in the intimate processes of our intellect.

Through these pages, we have traced the emergence of AI from theoretical frameworks to omnipresent forces in our routine affairs. We've seen how automation transcends the assembly line, ushering in an era of deep learning, predictive analytics, and smart technologies that tailor our experiences, safeguard our health, and optimize our time. The key theme reverberating throughout this narrative is adaptation: as automation assumes greater roles, the imperative for individuals, businesses, and societies to evolve with these changes has never been more critical.

The journey through this exploration has unveiled the dualistic nature of automation: an incredible resource that magnifies human potential, yet one that raises crucial ethical and existential questions about the future of employment, privacy, and identity in a machine-saturated tapestry of life. Reflecting on the stories and testimonies within, we absorb lessons on the pressing need for thought leadership and prudent policymaking that will navigate the trajectory of automation toward universal benefit.

'The world has changed,' declares this book with each

revelation, imploring us to look deeper into the interplay between artificial intelligence and the human spirit. As you, the reader, stand equipped with the newfound knowledge and perspectives gained, the challenge now is to engage actively in shaping the landscape of this automated world. The conversation continues beyond the last page, and the thoughts presented here are seeds for the emergent dialogue on our society's collective future.

Therefore, as you set down this book, carry forward the insight and understanding that while automation's tide is inexorable, it is the collective wisdom and conscious input of humanity that will determine the shape of our tomorrows. Let us step forward with intention, ready to be participants, rather than spectators, in the grand evolution beckoned forth by the age of automation.

ABOUT THE AUTHOR

Jon Adams is a Prompt Engineer for Green Mountain Computing specializing and focusing on helping businesses to become more efficient within their own processes and pro-active automation.

Jon@GreenMountainComputing.com

Printed in Great Britain
by Amazon